S0-ARM-798

Ken Done the art of design

Ken Done

the art of design

S.C.E.C.G.S.
ROSEBY
LIBRARY
REDLANDS

Powerhouse Publishing part of the Museum of Applied Arts and Sciences

Cover: Ken Done in front of *Walking through the Cabin garden, II, Nasturtium*, 1993, acrylic on canvas, 225 x 200 cm.

Design: Colin Rowan, Powerhouse Museum
Editing: Elizabeth Feizkhah
Translation: Kaoru Sato
Photography: Penelope Clay, Powerhouse Museum
Word processing: Anne Slam, Powerhouse Museum
Finished art: Catherine Dunn, Powerhouse Museum
Production: Julie Donaldson, Powerhouse Museum
Printing: Griffin Press, Adelaide

Published in conjunction with the exhibition
Ken Done: the art of design at the Powerhouse Museum
7 December 1994 – 7 May 1995.

ACKNOWLEDGMENTS

The museum gratefully acknowledges the assistance of Ken and Judy Done and Ms Chie Matsukawa of Gallery Tamon in Japan.

All paintings reproduced in this book are held in the collection of Ken and Judy Done unless otherwise acknowledged.

CIP

Ken Done: the art of design
Bibliography.
ISBN 1 86317 050 2
ISBN 1 86317 049 9 (pbk)
1. Done, Ken. 2. Done, Judy. 3. Graphic Arts — Australia.
4. Design — Australia. 5. Fashion — Australia.
760.092

© 1994 Trustees of the Powerhouse Museum

This book is copyright. Apart from any fair dealing for the purpose of study, research, criticism or review, or as otherwise permitted under the Copyright Act, no part may be reproduced by any process without written permission.

First published 1994
by Powerhouse Publishing,
part of the Museum of Applied Arts and Sciences
PO Box K346 Haymarket 2000 NSW Australia

Every effort has been made to contact the copyright owners of and provide correct acknowledgment for the illustrations in this book. All inquiries should be made to Powerhouse Publishing.

5/95 ERUDITION $29.95

031194

Contents

Forewords

Two years ago, in the depths of the recession, the Powerhouse Museum in Sydney opened a permanent exhibition on the subject of Australian success in industry and design. It was called *Success and innovation: achieving for Australia.*

Success and innovation is an exhibition for an Australian audience. It is designed to tell positive stories about Australian capabilities and to deny some of the recurring myths of Australian failure. One of these is that Australians can invent but are incapable of carrying out development. Another is that Australians are hopeless at marketing their products.

Done Art and Design was represented in the exhibition but only in a small way. A tray of four items was not an adequate representation of the products of a company doing business in a number of different countries; a company with a quite brilliant grasp of marketing.

The exhibition *Ken Done: the art of design* and this book produced as a companion to it, redress the balance and trace the history and successes of Done Art and Design.

The essays in this book each deal with a particular aspect of the Done story and seek to situate Done products within the context of Australian graphic design, textiles and fashion. In addition, two Japanese authors relate something of the impact of Done in the Japanese market and the way in which Ken Done is regarded in Japan. Having accompanied Ken to Japan, I know from my own experience that this is an unusual and highly interesting story.

Exhibitions are ephemeral experiences. Nobody expects or wants an exhibition to last forever, but any exhibition is ephemeral in a very special sense. It may sound obvious, but it is worth stating that exhibitions can only be experienced by visitors

Ken Done *Me*, 1984, oil on canvas, 191 x 184 cm, exhibited in the Archibald Prize, Art Gallery of New South Wales, 1985.

during their stay in the museum. In the case of the Powerhouse, the average length of stay is about three hours although, of course, some visitors stay much longer. In the case of the Ken Done exhibition, the length of the visit may well be increased by the time it takes to have a meal. This is because the museum's restaurant, entirely painted by Done, is an integral part of the exhibition.

But a publication is something that visitors take away with them. It can be read and studied at leisure over a period of time. It is both a memento and a record of the exhibition but it is also more. The interpretative and evaluative comments of the various authors, their tones of voice, are something with which our audience can engage. Readers, particularly students, will no doubt want to pursue topics themselves and discuss together issues surrounding Ken Done and his works.

There are mixed reactions to the work of Done.

His commercial success merits the approval and admiration of some, while others look askance upon it.

A particular issue for many is Ken Done's role as a painter, a fine artist. The exhibition and this book make it clear that there is an integral relationship between Done's art and the designs produced by him and his wife, Judy. This relationship is unique. Visitors to this exhibition and readers of this publication will be able to form their own evaluation of it and their own assessment of Done's contribution to Australian cultural life, and of the way he has shaped and altered perceptions of Australian culture in the minds of the citizens of other countries, particularly our neighbours on the Pacific rim.

Terence Measham

Director

Powerhouse Museum

8   Ken Done *Judy*, portrait of Judy Done, 1985, oil on board, 89 x 49 cm.

I recall the day Ken Done first visited Seiko Instruments' Takatsuka Plant, near Tokyo. There he saw how we produce watches. Each piece is assembled by a highly automated robotic system.

Ken was impressed and made the following comment: 'A watch looks so simple: a face, dial, hands and wrist strap. I never realised that such an advanced engineering system lay behind it. You must have made many innovations and devoted considerable effort to developing this system.'

'Ken,' I replied, 'your works also look simple. But they too require a lot of thought, creativity, and strenuous effort. That's what our professions have in common.'

Ken and I shook hands. That moment marked the beginning of our mutual understanding and friendship.

One of the characteristics of Ken's work is its combination of outward simplicity with deep underlying humanity and warmth. This is why it gives one a feeling of peace, happiness and hope, and why it is so popular internationally.

All of Ken's work expresses his caring personality and the warmth of his entire family. It also offers us an important philosophy: that we live for happiness and well-being and that art and culture enrich our lives.

We are indeed fortunate to have such art as Ken's. I am sure it will continue to be a source of pleasure and goodwill for people everywhere.

Reinosuke Hara

Vice President

Seiko Instruments Inc

Ken Done has produced artwork for five calendars and worked on other promotions for Seiko Instruments Inc including three filmed commercials.

Artist's statement

By definition, I suppose an exhibition of works in a museum must look backwards. And yes, the works in this exhibition do chronicle the last decade or so of things we've produced in both art and design. But clearly this exhibition shows influences long before the last ten years and, I hope, points to a long future of further development.

An artist/designer's work is really a history of all the things felt and seen along the way. Some rejected. Some cherished. For me some of the earliest images I can remember are those coloured pages in encyclopaedias where all the butterflies or birds or flags were shown. Or storybooks with beautiful illustrations.

I grew up in a little north coast country town. I loved the river, the sunshine, the birds, the sand. The colour of the sky. I loved painting pictures. And colouring them in. And showing them to my parents and friends. And that's what I still do.

The pictures have become more complex (I've now had over 40 solo exhibitions). The colouring in has become more detailed (I can even go over the lines!). And my family and friends have become an audience of many many thousands. Worldwide.

I've often felt that there is an artificially created division between 'art' and 'design'.

I feel that great 'art' always has strong 'design' elements. And that great 'design' can be seen as 'art'. But I'm not interested in a wide discussion about what constitutes great art or design. All I can vouch for is what I like.

All I've asked of an audience is that they should consider what problem it is that I was trying to solve.

The creation of a design for a piece of fabric that

Ken Done in the Powerhouse Garden Restaurant, 1994.

is to be printed in a limited number of colours and ends up on swimwear should be seen differently from, say, a painting about relationships that is to hang in a gallery. I try to do both with as much skill as I can muster.

In the area of design, it is often a creative process of collaboration with my wife, Judy. Or working closely with my assistants. When I am painting, though, I work alone.

I enjoy both activities. In my case, the stimulation of the number of activities we are engaged in has a very beneficial effect on my paintings.

I believe that I am a modern artist. Living in modern times. Using the modern skills of mass communication and international media. But as 'modern' as the business structure we have developed is, the act of painting has not changed much since cave painting in prehistoric times.

Then it was marks on a wall. Now it is work on a canvas. Or a garment. Or a poster. Or a film.

Most of the works in this exhibition could not have happened without my design partnership with Judy. Or the great contribution of our 'family' at Done Art and Design.

Most of the exhibition could not have happened without the commitment of Donna Lee Brien and the dedication and skills of the professional team of curators, designers and others from the Power-house Museum. And most certainly this exhibition could not have happened without the concept, direction and encouragement of the director of the Powerhouse Museum, Terence Measham.

I am deeply indebted to them all.

Thank you.

Ken Done

The Powerhouse
Garden Restaurant
painted by Ken Done

Terence Measham

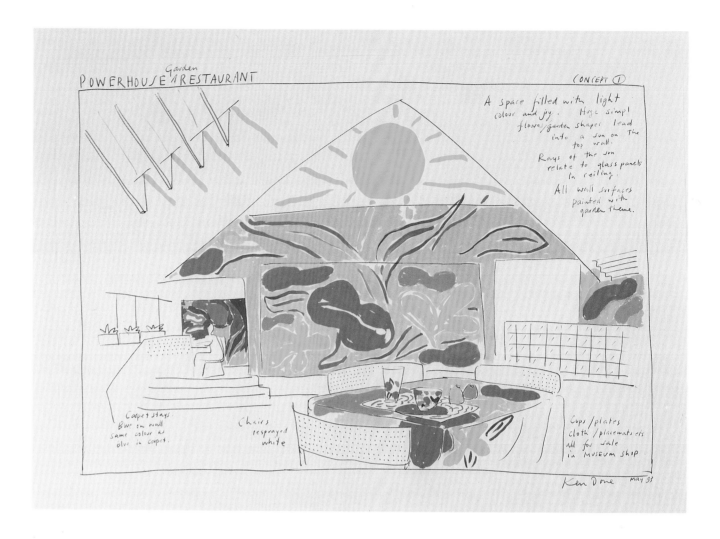

Ken Done's working drawings for the Powerhouse Garden Restaurant, ceramics, glassware and merchandise, presented to the Trustees of the Powerhouse Museum, 1993.

Six years after the Powerhouse Museum opened its doors, we decided it was time to freshen up the restaurant and also make it better known. The labyrinthine nature of the museum meant that the restaurant, tucked away on an upper level near the executive offices, was hard to find. Many of our visitors have come and gone unaware that it existed! Moreover, the restaurant was not exactly a colourful or glamorous facility. Rather, it was finished tastefully in a range of dark greys, darker greys and black. It gets little light most of the time. What was obviously needed was colour! And it needed a theme. Ken Done seemed the perfect answer. He is renowned for his highly colourful designs which express and celebrate the warmth and the joy he finds in Australian life. We asked Ken to discuss the matter with the Board of Trustees and he made presentations to them on a couple of occasions. The museum's idea was that the restaurant could be painted all over, walls and ceiling. Ken

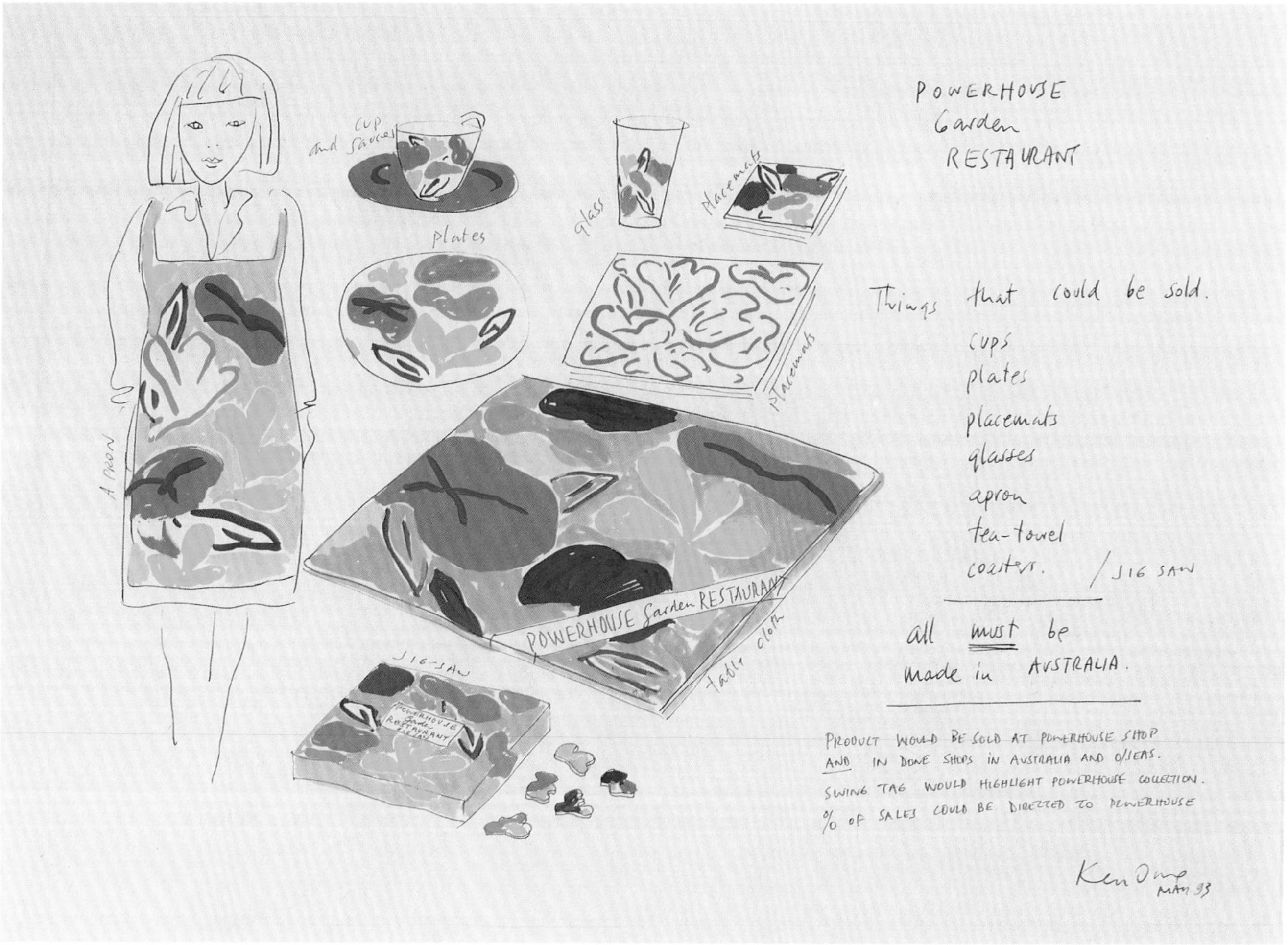
POWERHOUSE
Garden
RESTAURANT
Things that could be sold.
cups
plates
placemats
glasses
apron
tea-towel
coasters.
/JIG SAW
all must be
made in AUSTRALIA.
PRODUCT WOULD BE SOLD AT POWERHOUSE SHOP
AND IN DONE SHOPS IN AUSTRALIA AND O/SEAS.
SWING TAG WOULD HIGHLIGHT POWERHOUSE COLLECTION.
% OF SALES COULD BE DIRECTED TO POWERHOUSE
Ken Done
MAY 93
cup and saucer
plates
glass
placemats
placemats
APRON
JIG-SAW
POWERHOUSE Garden RESTAURANT
table cloth

suggested the theme of a garden which would alleviate the somewhat oppressively industrial character of this part of the Powerhouse's extensive range of buildings. A garden theme, he thought, would provide energy by the tension or counterpoint it would set up against the massive brick walls of the old Turbine House and the adjoining Boiler House. Initially, Done provided an idea of his scheme in miniature by working on a scale model of the restaurant, complete with lift-off roof, provided by the museum's superb model-maker, Iain Scott-Stevenson. This was presented to the Trustees, who gave it their assent.

Done took his theme from the quite extraordinary terraced garden that he and Judy Done had developed above their 'Cabin' on Chinamans Beach in Sydney. Both garden and cabin have provided inspiration for Ken Done's creativity over many years. The Cabin is, in fact, a pleasant, well-appointed cottage at the water's edge on a placid reach of Sydney

Harbour. In addition to the stepped garden with its steeply descending rocky path above the Cabin, there is a flat area, almost at water level, where the Dones entertain their guests and play *boules*.

The Cabin itself and this flat part of the garden form a modest composition, although superlatively located. What has intrigued me ever since I first visited the place is that the cabin and its piece of foreshore seem like a quotation straight out of the life of Pierre Bonnard. To a considerable extent, the interior of the Cabin resembles the interior of the small villa Bonnard bought at Le Cannet in the south of France in 1925. But much more than this, the Cabin resembles an inland refuge belonging to Bonnard on the banks of the river Seine at Vernonnet. Just as Ken Done calls a perfectly livable, if modest, dwelling a cabin, so Bonnard called his place at Vernonnet 'Ma Roulotte' — my caravan. The similarities are even more acute. In paintings of 'Ma Roulotte' Bonnard shows a single tree — or rather tree trunk — around which domestic dramas took place. So it is at the Chinamans Beach cabin, where, again, a single tree punctuates activities on the lawn, whether *boules* or other pleas- antries, such as playing with Done's dog, Spot.

Even Spot is a quotation! Don't get me wrong. Spot is a real live creature much loved by the Dones and one who occasionally has to be persuaded out of the range of heavy metal during a game of *boules*. Spot is not a dachshund but he does seem to play the same role as the ubiquitous sausage dog in Bonnard's paintings. More than that, Spot seems like a quotation from David Hockney in *his* paintings of his dachshund, a conscious quotation by Hockney from the art and the life of Pierre Bonnard!

I don't believe for a minute that Ken Done has consciously imitated the lifestyle of Pierre Bonnard, even though there are in Done's paintings quite distinct and candid references to the French master (as well as to Matisse and to many Australian artists admired by Done). What is at issue here is that there are a number of similarities between the lives led by coastal Australians (which is most Australians) and French attitudes to life. The French, as we all know, enjoy good food, which they prefer to eat, whenever possible, out of doors. Bonnard, a post-impressionist, chose to paint bourgeois mores, middle-class activities, just as his forebears the Impressionists had done.

The Impressionist generation celebrated middle-class leisure pursuits in Paris, the Ile de France and French coastal resorts. So what it boils down to is that Ken Done celebrates in his pictures an Australian lifestyle much devoted to domestic values, such as good food and drink, and to fun on the harbour — all of which can be enjoyed and absorbed from his vantage point in and around the Cabin. Yachting forms a big part of Done's subject matter, just as it characterised much of the work of Claude Monet.

Yet this comparison between Done's painting

Ken Done *Long view of the Cabin I*, 1992, oil and acrylic on four canvas panels, each 151 x 201 cm. Private collection.

Fretwell Photography

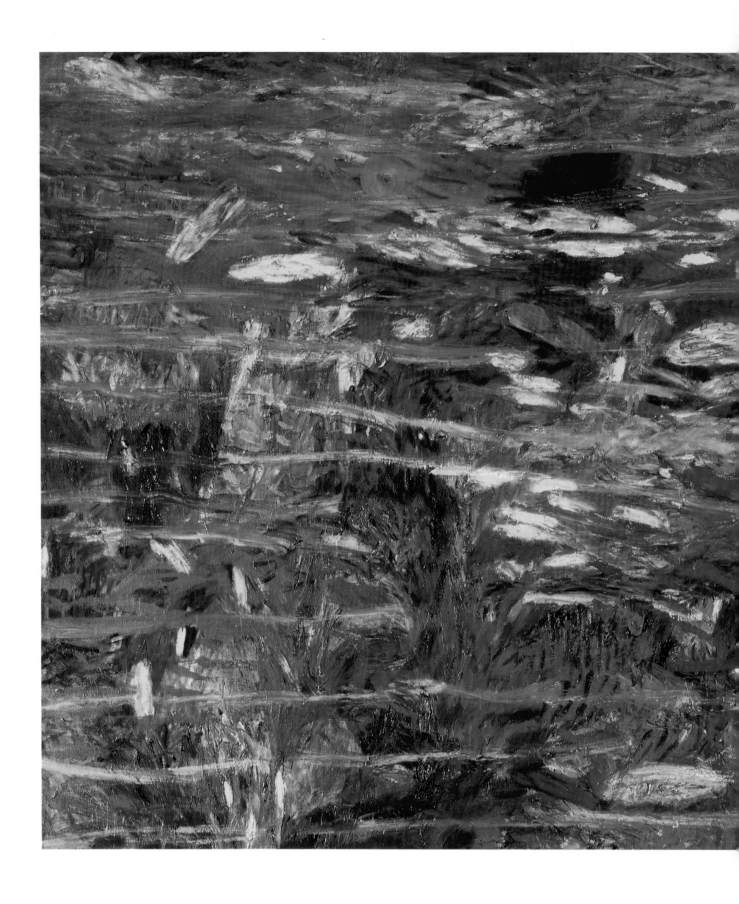

18   **Ken Done** *Listening to the fish*, **1990, oil on canvas, 161 x 206 cm. Private collection.** Fretwell Photography

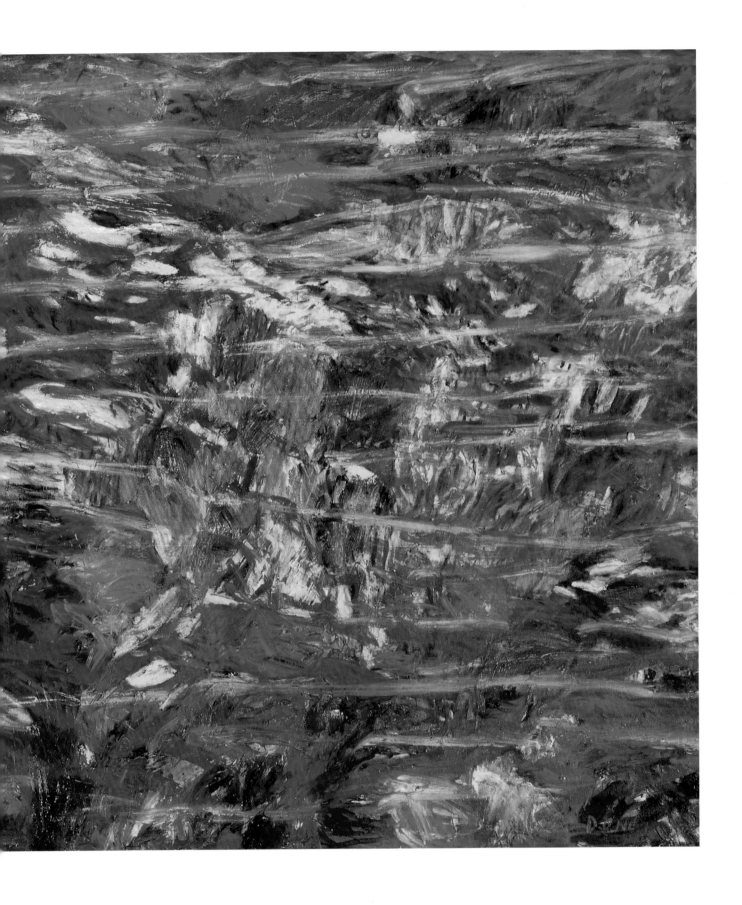

The Powerhouse Garden Restaurant

Ken Done *Thirteen oysters*, 1990, acrylic on paper, 39 x 45 cm. Fretwell Photography

output and French art can be misleading. It does not explain the considerable success Done's work achieves in Asia and in Japan. His Japanese audience views Done's work from an altogether different perspective. Their frame of reference leaves out of account the French connection of which we Australians are perhaps too acutely conscious. Japanese viewers recognise Ken Done as frankly and simply Australian. His bright colours they see as Australian, not derivative of Fauve painting. This is certainly true of Ken Done's reef paintings, which have no real French prototype, although with their different 'depths' and reflections they show a passing resemblance to and pay homage to Monet's *Nymphéas*.

The problem for Done is that the Australian art world has for a long time viewed the environment through brown-tinted spectacles. On my own arrival from Britain in 1980, I was solemnly assured that Australian colours were ochres and muted greys. I had great difficulty matching this advice with the brilliant, high-pitched and saturated hues that danced in front of my eyes. And *that* was in Canberra!

Japanese and Korean viewers express profound admiration for Ken Done's brilliant colours, which they find astonishing and extremely daring. That is because up there in the northern Pacific there is a strong emphasis on tones, on blacks, greys and whites.

At the Powerhouse Garden Restaurant, Ken Done's vivid shapes and colours flow across all surfaces; not just the walls but across the ceiling. The effect of this is to enliven and energise the architectural interior by denying it. There is no 'filling in' of architectural panels, which would be tedious, would provide an effect of inertia. Rather, Done uses the architecture in a dynamic and witty manner. For example, a peculiar feature of the room is that where the pitched ceiling meets vertical walls, there is a series of steps which articulate the join or angle. It is rather like an elaborate but internal string course. Done takes this stepped feature and turns it into the serrated edges of his giant green leaves and fronds.

This play with real and illusory space and form is carried on through a number of freestanding flat cut-out sculptures of vases and flowers, which are displayed ornamentally in different parts of the restaurant. To continue his game of illusion further, Done hung paintings at various points on the already-painted walls. Part of this playfulness had long-term intent. Done took the modest view that the museum might one day wish to paint over the restaurant — in which case, these separate paintings could survive and be kept as mementos of the whole scheme.

Users of the restaurant, however, while perhaps being unaware of Done's sensitivity and ethical approach, will nonetheless enjoy the scintillating play of imagery, in all its different layers, that energises their surroundings.

The Powerhouse Garden Restaurant

As already noted, the restaurant gets little sun. It gets none at all in the winter. These climatic conditions were explained carefully to Done at the outset. His obliging response was to paint a gigantic yellow sun in the gable over the south wall of the restaurant, with liquid rays of sunlight radiating across the pitched ceiling.

This great sun enhances the architectural characteristics of the restaurant by revealing and accentuating its scale. It does this by drawing attention to the height of the south wall. This in turn draws the gaze up and across what

is often called in Australia the 'cathedral ceiling'.

There is a well-known precedent for the Ken Done restaurant scheme. This is the Rex Whistler restaurant in the Tate Gallery, London. Whistler carried out this commission in 1926–27 with the title 'In pursuit of rare meats'. It is, in fact, a landscape fantasy. However, the painting is confined, frieze-like, to the walls of the restaurant. It is a horizontal scheme. It is pleasing that Ken Done has transcended the limits set by Whistler by undertaking to transform the Powerhouse restaurant as a

whole. But it is also pleasing that Whistler's work is reminisced, or at least reflected, at the Powerhouse. The Whistler murals are now almost 70 years old, yet still pull in the crowds (despite having been completely submersed in the Thames flood of 1928!). There is no reason to suppose that the Done scheme will not last as long or longer. It certainly pulls in visitors, who enjoy the experience he has provided and who commit themselves noticeably to longer meals and a great sense of occasion.

Painting and sculptures by Ken Done in the Powerhouse Garden Restaurant, 1994.

Interior looking up at ceiling, Powerhouse Garden Restaurant, Powerhouse Museum, Sydney, 1994.

Ken Done: the art of design

The Powerhouse Garden Restaurant

Ken Done's graphic design

Anne-Marie van de Ven

Today Ken Done is a prolific painter, but he has also had a long and successful career in advertising as an art director and as a graphic designer. During the 1980s he became famous for creating a huge industry in which his artistic ideas, motifs and even whole drawings and paintings were incorporated and translated into designs for use on mass-produced items from T-shirts to umbrellas. By retaining close control over the processes of design adaptation and reproduction, Done has been able to maintain a proprietary, almost painterly relationship to his design work.

Done's fame rests largely on his instantly recognisable graphic style, whose most characteristic features are the use of images that colourfully celebrate Australia and a bold incorporation of hand lettering. His lively renditions of the Sydney Harbour Bridge, the Opera House, sailboats, the beach, fish, flowers, kangaroos and koalas, combined with his use of a simple, childlike script both to sign and to caption his work, add up to a distinctive look which says both 'Ken Done' and 'Australia'.

A case in point is Done's AUSTRALIA sculpture for the Australian Pavilion at World Expo in Brisbane in 1988. Its boldly patterned letters are alive with Done's distinctively Australian symbols. The Southern Cross, smiling sun, palm tree, water, and patterns borrowed from

Done's signed and hand-lettered title for *Hanako*, the Tokyo women's magazine which has featured Done's art work on the cover of each issue since its inception in 1988. Reproduced courtesy Magazine House, Tokyo

(Right) Early art work for Done's AUSTRALIA sculpture at the entrance to the Australian Pavilion at World Expo in Brisbane in 1988.

Ken Done: the art of design

Ken Done's graphic design

It couldn't be simpler . . .
You walk into a bar, ask for "Bacardi
and Coke," and dream about the
Bahamas. The clearest water in the
world. But Bacardi rum is pure and
clearer than the Caribbean itself.
Most of Britain's Bacardi comes
from Nassau. 4,362 miles. Yet it still
costs only 53/9* a bottle. And mixes
beautifully with most things. Tonight,
have fun. Bacardi rum is the spirit of
adventure.

Bacardi Rum advertisement art-directed by Done in the Bahamas during 1967 for J Walter Thompson, London, in which he and his wife, Judy, modelled for the photographer, David Lowe. The sense of intrigue and adventure was motivated by the contemporary vogue for James Bond movies. Reproduced courtesy Bacardi-Martini Pacific Pty Ltd

Done working as creative director on a Johnson & Johnson shampoo advertisement in Sydney during the late 1970s. Water has been a recurring theme in Done's art and advertising for many years.

Aboriginal art seen in the early sketch on page 29 also appeared in the final work.

Deliberately simple in design and layout, and joyfully parochial, Done's look is so un-mistakably his own, and has become so popular with Australians and tourists alike, that his designs themselves —- and the signature 'Ken Done' — have become a kind of artistic trademark. This style took many years to evolve, and Done acknowledges numerous influences from the world of advertising to that of fine art.

Like many other Australian designers, Done started out looking to overseas models and felt it necessary to travel overseas to work and learn. During the postwar period, young Australian designers began to shift their attention from Britain to the United States.

One of Done's clients at this time was *Bandstand*, Australia's first television program to feature popular music; in creating the titles Done was influenced by the handwritten titles created by American designer Saul Bass for the film *The man with the golden arm* of 1956.

Brett Whiteley (Australia 1939–92) *The balcony 2*, **oil on canvas, 203.5 x 364.5 cm, 1975. Whiteley's paintings and calligraphic renderings of Sydney Harbour from his Lavender Bay retreat were an acknowledged source of inspiration for Ken Done's own Sydney Harbour drawings.** Purchased 1981, Art Gallery of New South Wales. Photograph courtesy Art Gallery of New South Wales. Reproduced courtesy Arkie Whiteley and Wendy Whiteley

The advertising design studio that Done established in Rowe Street, Sydney, in the early 1960s, shared the name of the American design journal *Visual Communications*. In the Australian Industrial Artists Association Annual *Advertising Art and Design* of 1963 Done was listed as a graphic, product, display, package and advertising designer as well as an illustrator, a typographer and a television graphics designer.

Around this time, the world of advertising was changing under the influence of television, the proliferation of colour magazines, and the growth of a sophisticated consumer culture. At the same time, the predominant graphic style was also changing from the uncluttered aesthetic of prewar Modernist forms to a more colourful, experimental approach led by the United States. This was the moment of Pop art, which rebelled against artistic elitism, embraced mass production and colour-magazine printing techniques, and used imagery drawn from

This early screenprint by Ken Done became his classic Sydney Harbour image reproduced on the first Done T-shirt.

Ken Done's graphic design

advertising, comic strips, film and television. The British artist Richard Hamilton described Pop as 'popular, transient, expendable, low-cost, mass-produced, young, witty ... and big business'. The Pop sensibility readily found a home in graphic design, where its leading exponents were Milton Glaser and the Push Pin Studio in California. Their pseudo-naive graphic style, incorporating Pop colours and imagery, became the defining look of the 1960s, and was a powerful influence on the young Done.

In 1965 Done, already oriented toward the United States in particular and an inter-nationalist outlook in general — thanks in part to his exposure to publications like *Visual Communications*, *The Saturday Evening Post*, and the *New York Art Directors Annual* — travelled to America. He freelanced briefly for McCann-Erickson in Los Angeles and was hired by the New York office of international advertising giant J Walter Thompson, but was unable to obtain permission to work in the USA.

Done moved on to J Walter Thompson's London office, where — at the height of the 'swinging '60s' — he worked as an advertising art director. He wrote, designed, directed and produced many advertisements in which he integrated film, photography, scripts, type and layout. Over the years Done received numerous awards for his advertising work, including the London Designers and Art Directors Cinema Campaign of the Year award in 1968 for his Campari cinema commercial.

Silk Ken Done scarf *(left)* with Sydney Harbour design of 1988 and *Douglas Annand looks at Sydney* scarf *(above)* from around 1950 by Annand. MAAS 85/1761. Annand scarf reproduced courtesy Mr Tony Annand

Ken Done's graphic design

The atmosphere of Sydney Harbour in celebratory mode was also captured by Martin Sharp, a contemporary of Done, for his *Festival of Sydney* poster of 1981. Reproduced courtesy Martin Sharp and the Sydney Festival and Carnivale. MAAS 90/166

(Right) Done's vision of Sydney's beaches recalls this poster depicting Bondi Beach designed by Percy Trompf for the Australian National Travel Association around **1935.** Photograph courtesy Australian Archives. Reproduced courtesy Australian Tourist Commission

TROMPF

AUSTRALIA

PARTICULARS AT SHIPPING AND TRAVEL AGENCIES

Ken Done's graphic design

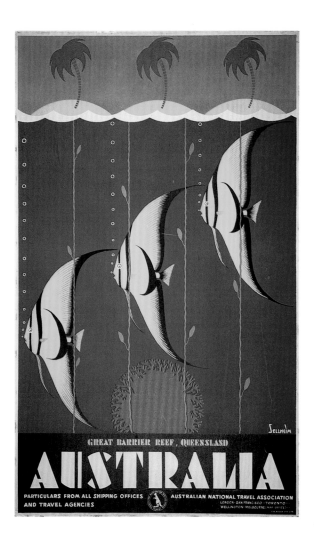

Poster, *Great Barrier Reef*, designed by Gert Sellheim for the Australian National Travel Association around 1939. Photograph courtesy Australian Archives. Reproduced courtesy Australian Tourist Commission and Mr N H Sellheim

Poster, *The Great Barrier Reef, Australia*, designed by Eileen Mayo for the Australian National Travel Association around 1956. Photograph courtesy Australian Archives. Reproduced courtesy Australian Tourist Commission

Done's *Barrier Reef Garden* design inspired a variety of products from posters to placemats. This image was taken from a poster advertising Done's Moore Park Gallery in Sydney. MAAS 91/1338

Ken Done's graphic design

FREE

So the Billy Blue masthead is at the bottom of the page. Nobody's perfect. It's there because we didn't want to plant it over Ken Done's archetypal view of Sydney. And next month Billy Blue may have another logo, anyway. This view of Sydney is now available in 100 sheet note pads on a smaller sheet size. To find out next to nothing about that see the ad on page 38.

Billy Blue

Ken Done: the art of design

By the time Done returned to Australia in late 1969, to rejoin J Walter Thompson in its Sydney office, two important themes had taken hold in his thinking. His travels to Tahiti, Mexico, Portugal, Turkey, Greece and Nepal, as well as to Japan, the US and Britain, had convinced him that Australia too could be marketed as an 'exotic' location and reminded him of the elements of this country's life and landscape that made it unusual and interesting. In addition, Done's experience in advertising had shown him the graphic and communications potential of multiplying images and of combining image and text with the company's or artist's trademark. He also strongly believed that there was essentially no difference between good original advertising art and 'high art'. Done has long identified with Australian painters such as Lloyd Rees, Sidney Nolan, William Dobell and Brett Whiteley, all of whom worked in the advertising industry before establishing themselves as artists.

By 1980, the Ken Done 'look' had taken shape. Its characteristic imagery was inspired by vivid memories of a happy Australian childhood and, later, by beach, harbour and garden views from his painting studio at Chinamans Beach. Harbour images have long been a popular subject for artists and designers alike and can be seen in works by the Smith and Julius Studios (Australia's 150th Anniversary Sydney 1938 poster), Douglas Annand (*Douglas Annand looks at Sydney* scarf), Brett Whiteley (*The balcony 2*), and Done's contemporary

(Left) Cover design for *Billy Blue* magazine featuring an early oil crayon drawing of Sydney Harbour by Done. Multiples of Done's Australian graphics were offered for the first time in this magazine. Reproduced courtesy Billy Blue Design

Mid 1980s beach towel design by Done featuring Sydney Harbour at night with the Harbour Bridge, the Opera House, the city and fireworks.

Ken Done's graphic design

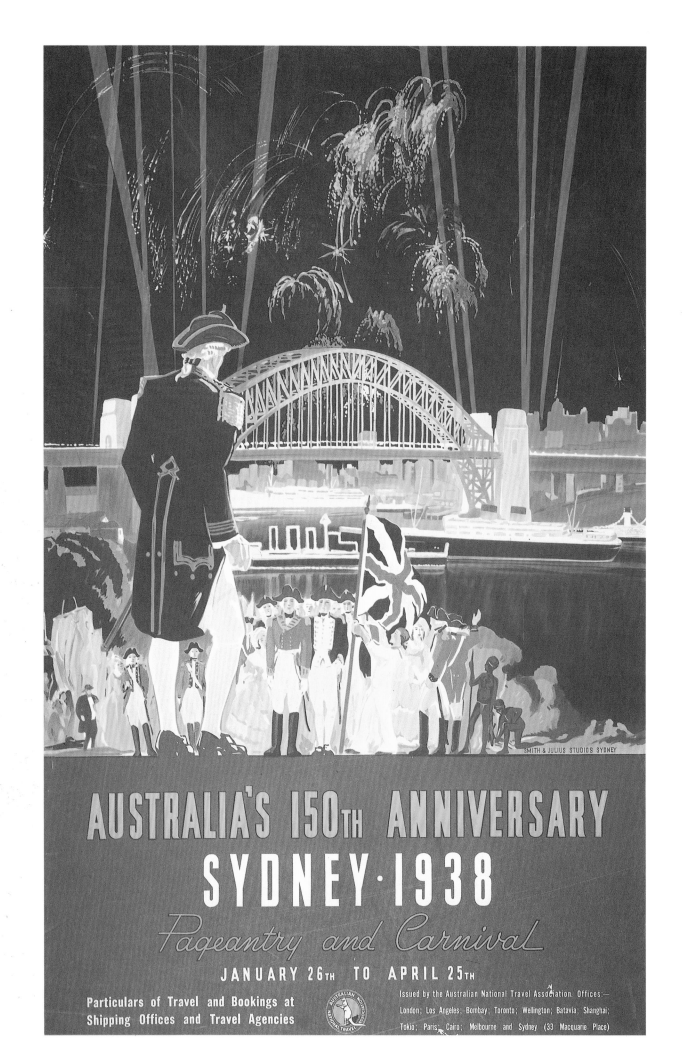

Martin Sharp (1981 Festival of Sydney poster). Done's later Barrier Reef imagery is also reminiscent of travel posters of the 1930s and '50s by Percy Trompf, Gert Sellheim and Eileen Mayo. Done's style, his choice of subjects, his bold use of colour and pattern, and his compositions owe something to influences as diverse as Flemish still-life painting, the South Pacific works of Paul Gauguin, paintings by David Hockney and Henri Matisse, the Australian landscapes of Fred Williams, and American and Australian naive art generally.

Done's bold use of vivid colour, while an important part of his distinctive graphic style, has antecedents in Brett Whiteley's saturating use of ultramarine blue and in the flamboyant fashion designs of Jenny Kee and Linda Jackson, who received the Fashion Industries of Australia Lyrebird award in 1977, shortly before Done began manufacturing his own leisure wear.

The public's first sight of the Done look, and first encounter with his 'art for the market' approach, was in 1980, when, to promote the solo exhibition of his paintings that opened his Art Directors Gallery in North Sydney, he silk-screened a sketch of sailboats on Sydney Harbour onto T-shirts. They sold briskly, and Ken Done the advertising man and painter had found a new outlet for his art. Done's work also became a fixture on the cover and in the pages of *Billy Blue* magazine, which promoted businesses and arts events on the North Shore.

Done's products during the 1980s often included a photograph of the artist. Oroton's packaging for a silk *Barrier Reef* scarf of around 1985 also featured promotional material about its artist/designer.
MAAS 91/1355. Reproduced courtesy Oroton International Ltd

(Left) **The Sydney Harbour Bridge with fireworks also featured in the Australian National Travel Association's celebratory poster for Australia's 150th Anniversary, Sydney 1938, alongside a sesquicentenary tableau depicting Aborigines 'welcoming' Captain Cook. Coincidentally, Done's first job was as an artist with the Smith and Julius Studios, the producers of this poster.**
Photograph courtesy Australian Archives. Reproduced courtesy Australian Tourist Commission

Ken Done's graphic design

As an unofficial ambassador for Australian tourism, Done designed numerous items featuring images which promoted specific locations or events such as this *Sydney Harbour 1998* carry bag produced by The Ink Group *(right)*. The Done bag introduced in 1990 *(above)*, on the other hand, simply displayed a bold Done signature on a characteristic yellow background. Reproduced courtesy The Ink Group Publishers

From 1980 on, Done's business grew as rapidly as the popularity of his graphic design. Ken Done Down Under (later Done Art and Design) began transferring his art and graphics, or licensing their transfer by other companies, onto fashion garments and associated products — from swimming costumes and umbrellas to bed linen and placemats. Kosta Boda, Sheridan Textiles, Hale Imports, Oroton International, The Ink Group Publishers and Robbie Cranfield all licensed his designs for use on their products.

The explosion in Done's popularity both contributed to and benefited from a surge in Australian national pride, most graphically demonstrated in Mojo's aggressive 'Down Under' marketing campaign for the Australian Tourist Commission (featuring the actor Paul Hogan) in the years preceding the 1988 Bicentenary celebrations, and in Done's own 'Down Under' label. In reinventing the popular iconography of Australia, Done helped define the country for Australians and tourist visitors alike — and his approach to marketing turned that iconography into a portable, wearable statement: 'This is where I come from' or 'This is where I've been.'

This reinvention, together with Done's idiosyncratic graphic style, has helped him become one of a very few Australian designers — including Sydney designer Douglas Annand, Melbourne designer Richard Beck, and, more recently, the young industrial designer Marc

Sydney Harbour 1988
Ken Done

Ken Done's graphic design

Naturally sparkling from the center of the Earth, France.

AMT 0146

Newson — who have been able to obtain important international commissions and command top fees for their original work.

Done won particularly enthusiastic recognition in Japan, where highly sophisticated graphics have been mass produced since the woodblock *ukiyo-e* prints of the 18th century. Done admires the Japanese aesthetic, in which art is integrated into every aspect of daily life and takes many of its themes from the natural world. In turn, the Japanese — who consider light-heartedness and happiness to be entirely appropriate, even desirable qualities in works of art — admire the freshness and seeming spontaneity of Done's painting and illustration.

In 1988 Done was commissioned to create artworks for the covers of *Hanako*, a weekly women's magazine based in Tokyo. His covers reveal the wide range of Australian subjects he has tackled and recall the wonderful artist-designed covers commissioned in the 1930s by Sydney Ure Smith for *The Home*, Australia's most sophisticated magazine of its time.

In 1991 Done produced the logo and artwork for East Rosetown, a new city near Osaka established by the Keihan Electric Railway Co. He also designed the can for the Australian-style beer Nouveau, made by the giant Japanese brewer and distiller Suntory, publicity brochures for the Japan Travel Bureau and phone cards for NTT (Nippon Telegraph and Telephone).

Done's approach to design and marketing, and

(Left) **Done quoted a professional fee of $1250 per finished crayon lithograph used by Monahan Dayman Adams advertising agency for the Perrier advertisements. The Perrier campaign went on to win the Certificate of Creative Excellence in the CLIO Awards of 1982.**
Reproduced courtesy Nestlé

Ken Done's graphic design

the demand he created for identifiably Australian consumer products and clothing, has influenced, inspired and paved the way for a number of other Australian design groups. These include Jumbana Designs in South Australia and Desert Designs in Western Australia, which translate images and motifs from Aboriginal art into a contemporary graphic style suitable for reproduction on clothing, accessories and tourist merchandise. Weiss Art, an offshoot of the Weiss fashion house, produces a range of clothing and linen featuring calligraphic black-and-white koalas, wombats, echidnas and the Sydney Harbour Bridge by Faye Wilson. This has enjoyed success in the United States, Britain and Japan. The clothing company Mambo, whose original products were T-shirts and board shorts for surfers but which now manufactures a range of clothing and fabrics for an international market, initially screenprinted some of Done's designs. Its 100% MAMBO label, launched in

50

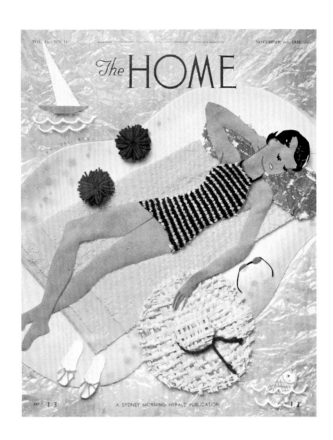

1985, has featured the work of graphic artists such as Matthew Martin and Reg Mombassa. The unconventional, even aggressive nature of Mambo's imagery does not appear to have hindered its acceptance by locals, tourists, or consumers overseas.

Ken Done has achieved an important place in the history of Australian design. When he started his career in 1959, graphic design barely qualified as a profession in this country, and most designers were led by overseas trends.

Ken Done's graphic design

The *Hanako* magazine covers featuring Done's artwork are reminiscent of the artist-designed covers produced for *The Home* magazine, published in Sydney from 1920 to 1942. *The Home* cover of 1 November 1935 *(above)* used the work of Sydney designer Dahl Collings. Reproduced courtesy Magazine House, Tokyo, John Fairfax Group Pty Ltd and Geoffrey Collings

Today, graphic design for advertising and for consumer products is a vibrant industry which not only brings in export income but helps define Australia both to itself and to the rest of the world.

References

Australian travel posters, Josef Lebovic Gallery, Sydney, 1990.

Advertising art and design, Australian Commercial and Industrial Artists Association Annual, 1963–64.

Caban, G, *A fine line: a history of Australian commercial art*, Hale & Iremonger, Sydney, 1983.

Friedman, Mildred and Freshman, Phil (eds), *Graphic design in America: a visual language history*, Walker Art Centre, Minneapolis and Harry N Abrams Inc, New York, 1989.

Haughton James, R, *Commercial art*, Longman, Green & Co, Melbourne, 1963.

'Ken Done by Ken Done', *The Sydney Weekly*, 24–30 May 1994.

Moodie, Ann-Maree, 'A different shade of Done', *The Australian Magazine,* 6–7 March 1993.

Sheill, Annette and Stephen, Ann (eds), *The lie of the land*, National Centre for Australian Studies, Monash University in association with the Powerhouse Museum, Sydney, 1992.

Trading places: Australian travel posters 1909–1990, Monash University Gallery and the National Centre for Australian Studies, Monash University, Clayton, 1991.

(Left) **Done's art is now adapted to fashion by his wife and partner, Judy. The swimming costume and bag featured on the *Judy Done Summer 1994–95 catalogue* have been adapted from Done's painting *Evening frangipani*, 1993.**

Ken Done's graphic design

Japan Travel Bureau brochure of 1989 featuring Done's illustrations, a portrait of the artist and a detail from his 1987 painting *Chinamans in summer*. Reproduced courtesy Japan Travel Bureau

(Left) **Done's poster design of 1991 for East Rosetown, a city owned by Japan's Keihan Electric Railway Co, adds a human dimension to the urban metroplis and promotes a healthy, happy and relaxed environment.** Reproduced courtesy Keihan Electric Railways Co

Ken Done's graphic design

The southern light

Yoshihisa Kinameri

58

Ken Done *Walking through the Cabin garden VII, lemons and clouds*, 1993, acrylic on canvas, 225 x 200 cm. *Walking through the Cabin garden*, a suite of fourteen paintings, was exhibited at Isamu Noguchi's Sogetsu Keikan (Hall) in Tokyo in 1993. It was installed as part of a collaboration with the architectural space and a sculptural ikebana designed by Mr Teshigahara, head of the Sogetsu School and a foremost Japanese contemporary artist.

When Ken Done began producing paintings for the cover of the weekly magazine *Hanako* in 1988, he immediately captured the artistic imagination of Japanese youth.

His southern-hemisphere colours permeated into every corner of the lives of young Japanese men and women during the economic boom. The world of Ken Done unfolded on a variety of items, from T-shirts to towels.

Done's art waves, with their trademark blue colour, eventually spread, like a *tsunami*, from a large island south of the equator to a small one the size of a dot.

The work of true artists knows no borders. And of course, the work of Ken Done crosses borders effortlessly. The vibrant surprise of his colours rids people of anxiety and makes them feel good. The light and shadow of the southern hemisphere, where he was born, differ slightly from those of the northern hemisphere. Those of the south have the effect of conferring life on every single being. Done's paintbrush differentiates those vivid colours and outlines with precise intuition. That is where his artistic god is enshrined.

Such a god has never known racial or national borders. For modern people, whose contact with different cultures has increased rapidly, there could be no gift greater than that. Truly international works are those that have the power to dispel the apprehension and inertia we sometimes experience when we encounter different cultures for the first time.

Done, who played an active role in large advertising agencies in London, New York and Los Angeles as an art director in the 1960s and '70s, must have gradually established his artistic identity during this period.

Borderlessness and the light and shadow of the south are the two elements that best account for the fascination of Done's art.

The blues of Picasso's blue period and Yves Klein's blue are two significant examples of the use of blue in modern painting. But Done's blue and the blue used previously in the history of art are completely different. If the blues in the works of Picasso and Klein represent sadness, hopelessness, ethics and impracticality, then Done's blue is free from worry, elitism or ethics. It has kindled a sense of human fellowship in an incredibly wide range of Japanese people, from youth to art journalists, the media, and international businessmen. This feeling of fellowship is becoming increasingly precious for humanity, which finds itself so aimless as it approaches the 21st century.

It is extremely difficult to provoke a sense of fellowship with a picture, but Done leaves not a trace of that effort in his finished works. And his work is so bold that it does not show any trace of emotions such as admiration and exaltation.

Such emotions are foreign to the sense of human fellowship. They are easily expressed but they take us nowhere. These days, a more complex response to art is required, and to

Artwork for Japanese telephone card with beach and ocean view designed by Ken Done for NTT (Nippon Telegraph and Telephone).

anchor it on canvas takes the precision of a brilliant forensic surgeon. Ken Done has chosen the hardest path in order to strengthen the sense of fellowship and humanity in his work.

Done is a fortunate artist, for he has been able to underpin his art with a strong boost in self-confidence as a result of the international stir he created right from his debut.

Whereas most other artists tend to be suspicious of the public, such a feeling will never hamper Done's work.

定価280YEN

Hanako

Ken Done

Ken Done

いい温泉旅館43軒で、美しくなる　大情報

いいリゾートホテル37軒で、気持よくなる

A級保存版　マハラジャもあわてて予約！

Tokyo's *Hanako* magazine, with a circulation of over 600 000, has featured Ken Done paintings on every issue since its inception in June 1988. This early *Hanako* cover from 1988 shows the deep rich light to be found in Done's beach and ocean illustrations. Reproduced courtesy Magazine House, Tokyo

From brush to bottom line

Richard Wood

Ken Done is one of a large and loose group of advertising 'creatives', businesspeople, fashion designers, filmmakers, actors, historians, politicians and social commentators who crafted a 'new' Australian image in the mid 1970s. Its hallmarks were the praise and use of vernacular language, motif and design in advertising, cinema, politics and literature. As a result overt 'Australianness' (albeit an Anglocentric, middle-class definition of it) became acceptable and popular.

By the early 1980s 'Australianness' had become an industry in itself; one which not only Australians but the rest of the world found extremely attractive. Consequently, during the economically mercurial 1980s there was a boom in the production and commercial success of Australian film, television, tourism and cultural products.

One of the maxims Ken Done formulated during this period, and one he has applied to both his painting and business ever since, was: 'We have to treat Australia as the centre of the world, and what we design in Sydney runs in California, Sweden, London ... because there's no reason why not.'

By the mid 1970s Done was at the pinnacle of a career in advertising. His art direction for television, cinema and press ads had received international acclaim; he had a harbourside villa at Chinamans Beach in Sydney and the best of everything in general, but it seemed to be leading nowhere. In 1980 Done, at the age

64

Done's first art-based product was hung from a tree to promote his art gallery.

The Art Directors Gallery, 4 Ridge Street, North Sydney.

From brush to bottom line

Done's contribution to the tourist-based koala cult of the 1980s.

of 40, decided to support his family through painting and drawing, with only a minimal income from freelance advertising work. In retrospect Done acknowledges how extraordinary this step was: 'It's very easy to risk everything when you've got nothing. I reckon it's a bit more complex to risk everything when you've got everything.'

Let the business begin

Most significant Australian industries have grown up around a single idea or product. In Ken Done's case this would have to be a T-shirt that hung from a tree in the front garden of number 4 Ridge Street, North Sydney in 1980, with the accompanying message, *Sydney Harbour T-Shirts $10 — Please come inside.*

The T-shirts were actually a promotional device for Done's first exhibition of paintings at his new Art Directors Gallery, intended as a showcase for advertising people's art. They were a sellout and Done soon realised that his future lay in a different way of selling his art. He recalls, 'Once I made the step of seeing that people would wear something as a piece of art, everything emanated from that.'

Done's next venture was a limited-edition poster of simple shell drawings that he hawked to shopkeepers in the comfortable Sydney suburb of Mosman, which takes in Chinamans Beach. Here shoppers were familiar with the beach and harbour themes that Done painted and were keen to acquire a fresh interpretation of them.

Barrier Reef colours transform glass into tropical fish for Kosta Boda.

Done's most decisive business move was to open a combined Art Directors Gallery and Sydney Harbour Shop in Sydney's tourist quarter of The Rocks in 1982. The parochial themes of his paintings and products — Sydney Harbour, the Opera House, the Harbour Bridge and sailboats — ensured that most tourists would link their visits with his product.

But it wasn't only tourists who became customers. Done's work appealed to ordinary Sydneysiders keen to celebrate and even brag about the distinctive beauty of their city.

Done's smiling grey koalas, painted with a few broad and lush brushstrokes, were translated to paper and textile products for sale in the shop in the early 1980s. They were snapped up by visiting Japanese tourists, keen to take home a likeness of their favourite Australian marsupial. This was an early indication of the Japanese appreciation of Done's work.

By 1985, the range of products emblazoned with Done's paintings included swimwear, resort wear, handbags, umbrellas, posters, jewellery, sunglasses and visors, homewares, sheets,

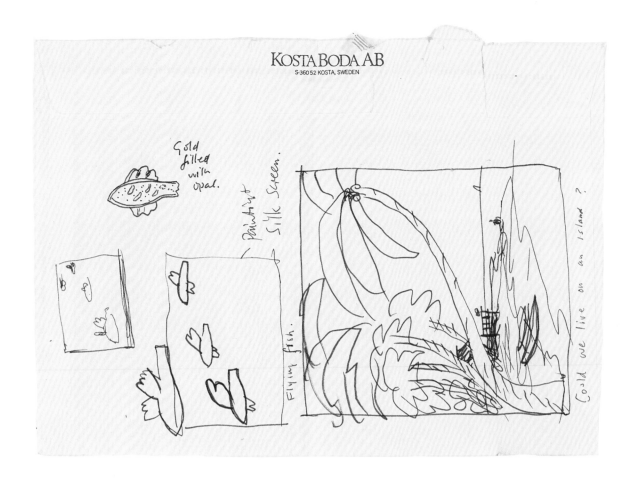

Drawings on an envelope captured Done's inspiration for the Kosta Boda glassware range.

towels, greeting cards and calendars. And in 1986 he launched the Art to Wear label, a fashion range developed by his wife, Judy, that is the mainstay of the Done business today.

Some critics insist that this mass production dilutes the artistic worth of Done's paintings. But his personal control and physical closeness to the processes and the people who manufacture his products ensure that his artistic integrity is present in the thousandth T-shirt or the millionth greeting card sold in his name. And his art now reaches a broader

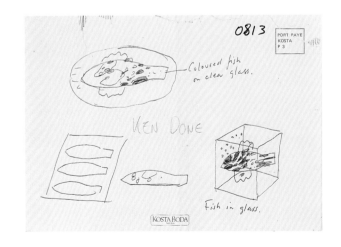

and larger audience than it could ever have done in the rarefied world of the art gallery and art dealer.

Done's paintings are the starting point for a remarkable Australian enterprise which now employs 160 people, indirectly supports thousands of others, and sustains a customer base of 150 000 a year. In 1992, stores in Japan, the United States and Australia were selling millions of dollars worth of fashion and other products to a loyal and expanding market.

At various times since the early 1980s, much of the company's income has come from commissions for art and design ideas for other manufacturers and from the licensed manufacture of Done Art and Design products in other countries. For example, in 1987, Kosta Boda, the Swedish glassmaker, commissioned Done to design a range of glassware based on his Great Barrier Reef paintings. The range was sold worldwide and included a range of fish sculptures and tableware.

In 1991 a Japanese beer, Suntory's Nouveau, was launched in a can designed by Done. This became perhaps the most reproduced of Done's works, with 80 million sold within two months of its release.

Perhaps more significantly, in 1992 the Australian biscuit manufacturer Arnott's honoured Done with a commission to redesign its famous parrot trademark. This was the Australian equivalent of being asked to redesign the Coca-Cola trademark. The limited-

(Above and right) **Suntory's beer cans, perhaps Done's most pervasive artwork to date.** *(Far right)* **Done's redesign of an Australian icon, the Arnott's biscuit tin and** *(top right)* **previous Arnott's biscuit tin.** Reproduced courtesy Arnott's Biscuits Limited

From brush to bottom line

The sincerest form of flattery? Done's influence on some Australian, Hong Kong, Italian and Greece manufacturers shines brightly from their products.

edition biscuit tins that bore Done's redesign sold like hot cakes; his $50 000 fee was donated to UNICEF.

Licensing the manufacture of products can be a lucrative avenue for Australian businesses which are too small or lack the infrastructure to produce large numbers of products for worldwide markets. In the 1980s Done Art and Design swiftly expanded into the United States and Japan by licensing the manufacture of T-shirts and other products bearing Ken Done designs in those and other countries.

The disadvantage of licensing is the loss of control it entails and the need for constant policing and assessment of product quality and authenticity. A series of breached agreements and poor products legally bearing the Done name have recently led the company to discontinue licensing agreements with all but a few Australian companies such as The Ink Group Publishers (greeting cards), Oroton International (handbags and accessories), and Sheridan Textiles (manchester), which have the capacity to serve both local and international markets.

Imitation may be a sincere form of flattery, but unlicensed and illegal copies of Done products have proliferated. Although the company has been swift to act wherever possible to stop copyright infringements, in South-East Asia copyright laws are widely flouted. One amusing example of this was a souvenir T-shirt bearing the message 'Gulf of Thailand' underneath

Judy Done works in the tradition of most fashion designers, first defining the fabrics to be used and their colourways, and finally sketching each garment.

Done's Sydney Opera House and Harbour Bridge design.

Done's continuing success is a measure of the validity of his approach to art, design and business. Contrary to the popular image of the deserving artist starving in a garret or living off the public purse, Done has proven that art and business can not only coexist but also nurture and inspire each other as well as their audiences.

Moyra Proudfoot is entrusted with transferring original paintings to the fashion and resort wear range.

The process at work from painting to product

The biggest-selling products inspired by Done's paintings are those in the fashion and resort wear ranges, the result of a complex interplay between the artist and designers, technicians and business managers.

Butterfly dreams (see pages 76–77) is the title of a painting exhibited in Australia, Japan and the United States, a range of fabrics, and two fashion ranges.

Inspired by a Japanese *haiku* poem of the same name, Done set out to paint, he says, 'an unbelievably pretty picture' to express the short

Proudfoot begins by tracing the selected part of the painting. She then colours it, reducing the original palette of thousands of colours to the handful that are viable for printing.

I would learn
of their dreams

in the flowers

but

ah!

Butterflies
have no

voice.

REIKAN

The original *Butterfly dreams* painting by Ken Done, 1989, four panels, acrylic on canvas, 122 x 372 cm. Fretwell Photography

花の夢
聞きたき蝶に
殻耳もなし

鈴翠

From brush to bottom line

Colour artwork for *Butterfly dreams* design prepared by Proudfoot. The myriad of colours used by Ken Done in *Butterfly dreams* had to be limited to a handful for the printing process.

life of a butterfly. He immediately recognised the painting's potential for transposition onto fabric. As he observes: 'You'd have to be extremely dull not to think, "Oh, that would make a nice piece of material".'

This process was led by Judy Done, who has 30 years experience in the fashion business and who designs and manages the fashion, resort wear and accessories range. Ken discussed each step with Judy and textile designer Moyra Proudfoot, who was responsible for turning this canvas into production artwork.

Butterfly dreams was one of nine different summer prints developed by Judy Done for the 1991–92 range. She had to imagine how the painting would look printed on or woven into fabrics. She had to imagine how it would move, how it would drape, what size it should be, whether it should be a repeated pattern or whether the painting should be printed in its entirety — even how it would look against the other summer prints in the shop.

Pattern-making and cutting are in-house activities of the Done organisation.

Garment assembly is subcontracted to Australian manufacturers.

Seeing into nature's heart

Machi Tawara

Once in a while it's good to exercise the parts of your brain you don't use regularly. It was autumn, the ideal time for reading, so, attracted by a beautiful cover, for a change I began reading a book of philosophy.

Some words that were quoted in the book lingered strangely in my mind. And hidden in these words, I thought I found the key to the fascination Ken Done's works hold for me — that mysterious something I had not quite been able to put into words. 'The mixtures that exist at the point of apparent difference are in fact innate in nature.'

Let me briefly explain the context in which these words appeared. Classical thought deliberately and carefully separated concepts such as 'good and bad', 'consciousness and nature'. On the other hand, romanticism focused on the mixtures which existed prior to this separation in order to view 'nature as it is'. The quotation came in a passage describing this romantic ideology.

The nature and scenes that Ken Done paints are precisely those mixtures, and are a part of 'nature as it is'. Done has never attempted to separate or extract one thing from another. On the contrary, his heart appears to be moving in the opposite direction. Done sees deeply into nature's womb, from which has come the life that unfolds before us, and into the subtle worlds that are concealed in the visible, tangible one. He lets us enjoy his visions, at times surprising us with his use of form and colour.

The sea, for example. Done paints it over and over again. How many expressions the beaches around Sydney have! It's as if a hundred exclamation marks are not enough to describe the variety on view. You can enjoy his *oeuvre* by making your way through all his seaside landscapes, or even by tracing the colours of his sea alone.

I'm reminded once again how much life and colour there are in the world. I tend to identify just one shade of blue with the colour of the sea, and I also tend to feel satisfied just framing the scenery before me as if I were taking a snapshot.

Let me recall the philosopher's words: 'The mixtures that exist at the point of apparent difference are in fact innate in nature.'

The book begins with a story of a postcard arriving from Australia. Coincidentally, that is Ken Done's home country. Perhaps it was this that set my thoughts off in this direction. But now these words strike me as having been written as a key to understanding Done's work, which makes me experience the source of life.

Ken Done once spoke in an interview about colours. He said: 'There isn't any single colour that I dislike. I like all colours. The only important thing is to express them beautifully by combining them in the right way. Artists have a duty to create their own harmony of colours.' 'I like all colours' — what courageous words! The more colours you have on a canvas, the harder it must be to create harmony.

Autumn

Fish and FUJI II

Ken DONE

秋の魚と富士

Ken Done *Autumn fish and Fuji I*, triptych (detail), oil and acrylic on canvas, 210 x 468 cm, 1991.

Seeing into nature's heart

Ken Done *Freshwater girls*, 1985, oil on board. Exhibited in Tokyo at the Seibu Gallery in 1988 and Laforet Museum in 1989.

Painters use colours as poets use words. 'I like all words' — now am I, a poet, able to say that? I thought for a moment. Whether words shine or fade depends on their user — that's what Done was telling me here. Loving all the words in existence, searching for the beautiful combination, and challenging oneself to create one's own harmony of words — that must be the matrix from which poetry that taps the source of life is born.

The book, Done's works, and poetry — it was a day in late autumn when these topics, which might otherwise have seemed completely separate, came together unexpectedly.

From *Yomiuri Shimbun* 22 January 1989

Ken Done *Kameido*, 1989, acrylic on canvas, 61 x 61 cm. Private collection.

Seeing into nature's heart

Artist and artistry

Donna Lee Brien

SELF PORTRAIT   PREPARING

Ken Done *Self portrait: preparing to paint I and II (right)* **1992, oil and acrylic on two canvas panels, joined, 199 x 204 cm.** Fretwell Photography

I always accepted that once I did my first T-shirts and calendars for The Ink Group, and my work was in wide circulation, that my education as an artist would be in public.

Ken Done, 1994

Working closely with Ken Done as his personal curator and biographer has afforded me the unique opportunity to study his work and processes, character and aspirations. If I had to find one word to describe Ken Done and the scope of his activities, I would choose 'artist' — defining an artist both as one who practises within the fine arts and one who makes an art of their craft. Done's diverse accomplishments as a painter, a designer, a businessman and a philanthropist combine elements of art and artistry.

Done defines himself as a painter. On almost any day of the year he can be found in one of his three studios producing paintings, sketches and drawings. A glance into his studios reveals canvases in various states of completion stacked against the walls and on the floor, leaning against easels and each other. Paintings of Australia, especially Sydney, renditions of his family and friends and the objects with which they surround themselves show that Done works within the genres central to Australian painting: landscape, seascape, portrait and still life. From these subjects he has, however, fashioned a set of private themes to which he returns again and again: the beach, the harbour, the reef, the garden, the family, the studio, the nude, and the self.

His compositions are arresting in their vibrant colour and bold imagery, but their most interesting feature is their relationship to Done's own life. These paintings record in intimate detail day-to-day events: family meals, a day spent windsurfing, diving or walking, holidays, the view from a favourite window, a dream. The works created in this celebration of the everyday form a visual diary of the artist's experience, his imaginings, and his at times idiosyncratic and humorous way of seeing the world. The focus is always on a combination of personal experience and the beauty of the natural world.

One of the themes to which Done has constantly returned is the Cabin, his studio at Chinamans Beach. Since the 1970s this small white weatherboard house at the water's edge, the view it affords of Middle Harbour, its interior spaces and its surrounding garden, have provided a central inspiration for the artist. *Sunday* (1982) captures the essence of what the Cabin and the harbourside mean to Done: space, ease, light, pleasure, colour and creativity. On the yellow work table in the foreground of this painting are laid out the artist's paraphernalia — tubes of paint, ink pots, brushes and palette, postcards, shells, a potted plant and flowers in a glass. The frangipani in bloom, draping luxurious leaves over the railing, links the Cabin interior to the view outside. This is how Australians prefer to live:

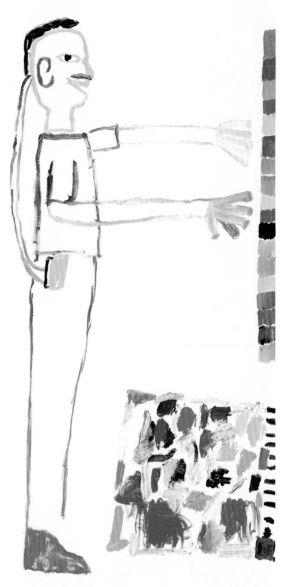

TO PAINT   KEN DONE 92

Ken Done in his Redfern studio, 1989. Photograph by Camilla Done

the inside outside; days on the terrace and the sundeck. The view of beach, foreshore, boats and bathers forms a painting inside a painting, a picture Done continues to paint from the same veranda over a decade later.

In 1982 Done recorded the scene in its minutest details, from the flecks on the shell's surface to the paint labels and the small white clouds on the horizon. By the end of the 1980s, the artist's reworking of this scene resulted in a series of images and visual signs — a personal pictorial language. In *Another Sunday I* (1989) Done has simplified the scene without losing any descriptive power. The work table still supports brushes, paint and the edge of a palette, but the garden has grown, and the frangipani and morning glories have been freed to float over a merging sea and sky. Triangular shapes signal boats, and the curves of frangipani leaves frame the entire composition.

In the 1990s Done is still returning to the Cabin for inspiration. The monumental suite *Walking through the Cabin garden* (1993) consists of fourteen panels (each 2 x 2.25 m) which together present a sweeping panorama of the Cabin's garden. The careful detail of earlier works has exploded into bold notations of flowers and saturated colours. In the panel *Morning glories* the colours and shapes alone identify these flowers, which have appeared in Done's painting since the late 1970s. As his business has grown, making increasing demands on his time and energies, the Cabin

has become a retreat where Done can turn away from the world, immersing himself in his own imagination. *Walking through the Cabin garden* is the result of such an escape.

Done approaches product design and marketing with the same creativity he applies to painting. One of his main achievements as an artist and designer has been to take the potentially prosaic subject matter and banal objects of everyday life and transform them into objects of beauty that seek to delight the senses. A pair of espadrilles jauntily sports paints and brushes; sunshine bursts from a tea towel; the morning glory T-shirt becomes an art form.

Only a few of Done's paintings are selected as the inspiration for the development of designs to decorate the fabrics and functional objects for which the name Done is best known. Their choice is sometimes deliberate, sometimes spontaneous: it might be based on the need for certain colours and shapes or be sparked by a momentary attraction to a painting hung in a gallery or an office. Paintings in their entirety are never reproduced on objects; instead they are adapted into designs suitable for decorative use. This adaptation often involves defining the numbers of colours and repeatable shapes and the sizes of images that will work on specific items. Thus a single panel from the four of *Butterfly dreams* (1989) was interpreted by the Done textile designer as a twelve-colour repeat pattern to be printed on fabric for use in a complete seasonal fashion range.

92

Ken Done *Walking the dog*, 1991, acrylic on board, 56 x 80 cm. Fretwell Photography

***(Left)* Ken Done *Blue vase, blue bowl*, 1987, acrylic on board, 76 x 51 cm.** Fretwell Photography

The Powerhouse Garden Restaurant project (inspired again by Done's Cabin garden) is another example of this process. The items designed and produced for use in the restaurant and for sale — dinnerware, manchester and clothing — allude to and reflect the shapes, patterns, colours and ambience of the painted environment, but do not replicate them. They were all designed as functional pieces which would complement, not copy, the overall decorative scheme. Done paints alone in his studio, but he worked with more than a dozen people to develop the Garden Restaurant's ceramics: a telling example of the collaborative effort that goes into the development of all Done products. Inspiring and coordinating the disparate talents of the Done organisation's more than 160 employees is a continuing exercise in sensitivity and good management.

Done has been active and creative in liberating the marketing of his work from existing systems. He firmly believes that 'In the times in which we live it is far too restricting to say that art can only be found in art galleries and not touch people's everyday lives.' His embrace and creative use of the commercial have enabled him to transmit this vision to a much wider audience than he could ever have reached by confining his work to established galleries or stores. While Done knows that art is inescapably a commodity, he has fostered a philosophy through his own galleries that exhibitions should reflect a passion and commitment to the works of art, rather than purely fiscal considerations. A unique feature of the Ken Done Gallery in Sydney's Rocks is the opportunity for visitors to see Done's studio and at times watch him at work. This enables Done to share with his audience the joys and excitement of the creative process — and reveals his openness to stimulation and comment.

The design company Done Art and Design, which fuses the complementary creative talents of Ken and Judy Done, is committed to promoting local achievement. Garments are designed and made in Australia using locally grown natural fibres, particularly cotton and wool. Judy and Ken do not wait to see what styles have been successful in Paris, Milan or New York before releasing their own products. Done fashions are produced for, and released first in, Australia and then marketed to the rest of the world.

Done traces his regard for Australia to his early childhood. He worshipped his father, who 'fought for Australia' in World War II. After his father's return, the family moved to Maclean, a small town in northern New South Wales, where Done remembers spending an idyllic Australian childhood of 'long hot summers, cicadas, the beach, floods, gum trees, jacarandas, burning cane and Saturday afternoon at the pictures'.

In his 20s, Done travelled to Japan and worked in advertising in New York and London. He felt an expatriate's pride in his country and, on returning home in the 1970s, began to paint

Ken Done *Dreaming of the moon*, 1990, gouache and oil crayon on paper, 63 x 47 cm. Fretwell Photography

Artist and artistry

images that compared Australia with what he had seen of other parts of the world. His work in advertising at that time involved major international accounts as well as iconic local brands such as Rinso and Radio 2JJ. From the first Sydney Harbour T-shirts in 1980 to today's sophisticated resort wear, Done has always seen his products as representing Australia to the world. His participation in initiatives promoting Australia, such as World Expo in Brisbane in 1988, the Sydney Olympic bid, Australian and state tourist commission programs, and the 'Australian-made' scheme, continue to manifest his support for and belief in this country.

Ken Done resists typecasting. Extremely adaptable, he can move with ease from painting in the seclusion of his Sydney studio to starring in a Japanese television commercial filmed in Tokyo. His passion for grasping the creative potential of the moment is also evident in the energy he devotes to his many charity projects. As Australia's goodwill ambassador for UNICEF, he has travelled to Africa and most recently Vietnam as spokesman in a documentary aiming to raise public awareness of aid projects in the country. Done does not feel the need to separate his different fields of endeavour. While filming in Vietnam under gruelling conditions, he recorded his journey in drawings. Upon his return Done completed a number of major paintings which, in conjunction with photographs by Peter Solness, formed the basis for an exhibition. All proceeds

from the show were donated to UNICEF.

Done experiences the world in terms of his emotions. He often speaks of the 'feeling' that he is trying to express through his work. 'I certainly work a great deal on simply how I feel about things,' he says. 'Not logic, not anything other than how I feel. If I had to describe how I go through life it would be that if something feels right I do it. My whole life has been like that, trusting in my emotions.' Done wants to communicate on this expressive level. The formal components of his paintings and the pro-cesses by which his designs are created and his products made are of course of great interest to Done himself, but he does not want them to be particularly noticed by his audience or customers. He prefers that others react purely emotionally to what they see: 'Often I have made paintings and products that seek on the simplest possible level only that the person looking at them should say, "Oh yes, that's beautiful".'

The Japanese art critic Shinichi Segi has recently identified this desire to create things of beauty as a utopian motivation: '[Done] tries to create a paradise — a paradise where one's hopes can be realised as best as humanly possible — not only as the artist's fondest dream but also as an ideal for humanity.'

Ken Done *Sunday*, 1982, oil on canvas, 102 x 82 cm. Fretwell Photography

Artist and artistry

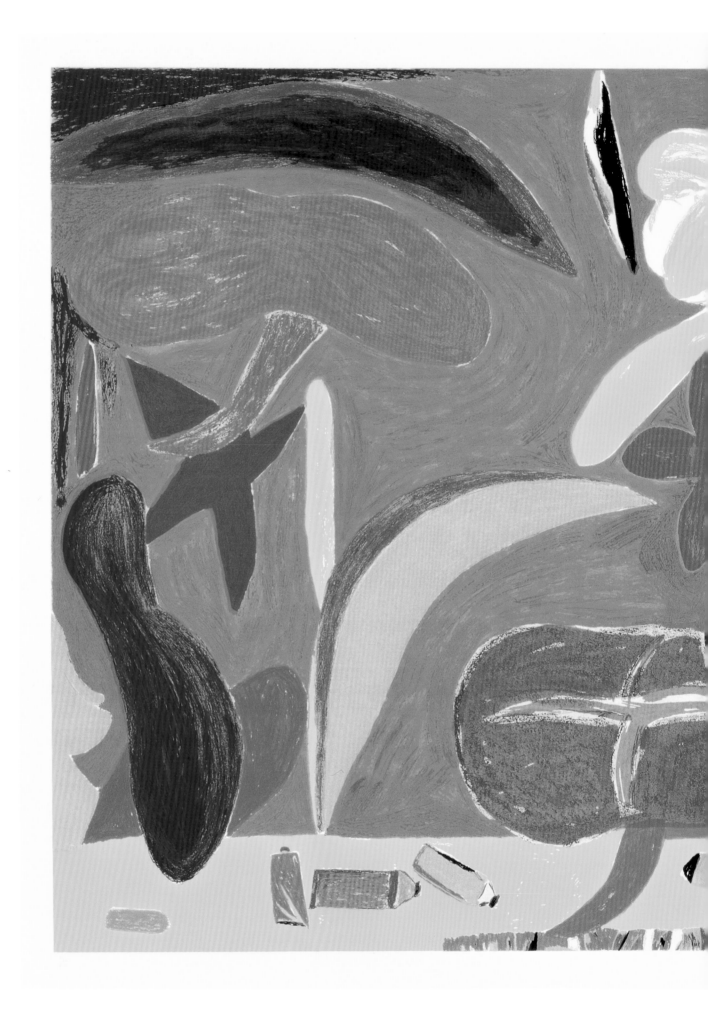

98   **Ken Done** *Another Sunday I*, **1989, acrylic on canvas, 122 x 18 cm.** Fretwell Photography

Ken Done: the art of design

Artist and artistry

Installation view of Ken Done's *Walking through the Cabin garden*, 1993, acrylic on fourteen canvas panels, each 225 x 200 cm,

Moore Park Gallery, Sydney, 1993. Fretwell Photography

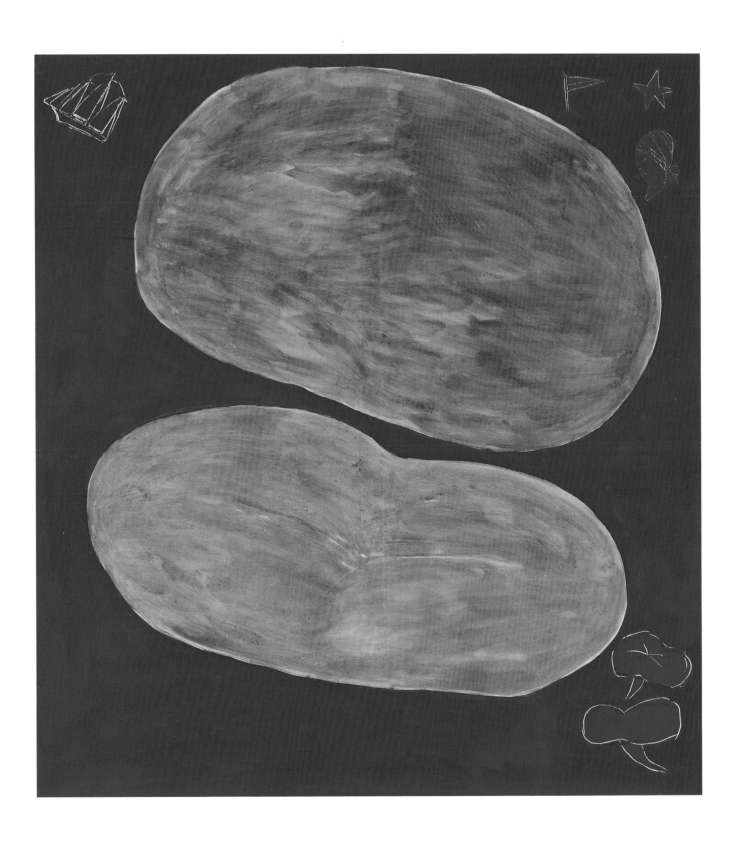

Ken Done *Walking through the Cabin garden, IX, Morning glories*, 1993, acrylic on canvas, 225 x 200 cm. Fretwell Photography

Done Art and Design *Butterfly dreams* **long-sleeved T-shirt, summer 1991–92, cotton.** Frontier Aviators

Done Art and Design *Paint-palettes espadrilles,* **winter 1993, canvas and rope.** Frontier Aviators

Ken Done *Butterfly dreams* (detail), 1989, panel one of four, acrylic on canvas, each 122 x 93 cm. Fretwell Photography

Chronology

Elizabeth Buzby

Childhood artwork, *Sunrise* and *Sunset*, about 1948.

Ken with fellow art students at East Sydney Technical College, 1959. *Back:* Vanessa Mason, Ken Done, Rosalind Fry; *front:* Felicity Ellison, Julia Mendel, Sylvia Parret. The *Sydney Morning Herald*, 15 October 1959. Reproduced courtesy John Fairfax Group

1950s

Ken

b 1940, Sydney

Somewhere my mother has a little painting I've done of the sunrise and sunset. Couple of boats, little house, sun going up, sun coming down. It's your life, isn't it? There's the sunrise, everything in between, and then you die ... hopefully on a nice day. — Ken Done

1954 enrols in National Art School, East Sydney Technical College

1959 hired by Smith and Julius Studios

Judy

b (Judy Walker) 1943, Sydney

1958 attends June Dally-Watkins School of Deportment

1958–60 works as a freelance model

● meets Ken while she is working in an advertising agency

Ken at the drawing board.

1960s

Ken

1960 appointed art director of Australian Applied Advertising

● opens his own studio, Visual Communications, in partnership with Bob Mitchell; its accounts include the television music show *Bandstand* and radio station 2GB

1962 visits Japan; meets with Tokyo Graphic Designers Association

1963–64 Visual Communications acquires accounts of Alitalia and BMC

1964 leaves Sydney for New York via Tahiti, Acapulco, Mexico City and Los Angeles, where he freelances for McCann-Erickson

1965 appointed art director, J Walter Thompson New York, but, lacking a work visa, leaves for London

In 1957 the J Walter Thompson Company billed nearly $300 million, roughly three-quarters of it in North America, the rest on the other four inhabited continents. The agency has 34 offices in 19 countries, and it is important in all of them.
— Martin Mayer, *Madison Avenue USA*, Penguin Books, 1961

● after working freelance, joins J Walter Thompson London

● marries Judy, who has arrived from Australia. They settle in Chelsea at the height of the 'swinging '60s'

1967 appointed art supervisor, J Walter Thompson London, where he art directs and appears with Judy in a Bacardi Rum commercial filmed underwater. This is the first time this technique has been used. Other accounts Ken handles include Silhouette swimwear, Campari, Bush Mills Irish Whisky, Gillette, and the Steel Company of Wales

1968 wins Gold Lion Award in Cannes for his art direction on Campari's cinema commercial

1969 wins London Designers and Art Directors Association Award, Cinema Campaign of the Year, for the Campari cinema commercial

● returns to Australia with Judy via Sweden, Italy, Greece, Lebanon and Nepal

Judy was often seen in the social pages.

(Right) **Ken designed his 21st birthday invitation**

107

Chronology

Ken and Judy in Sydney, 1962.

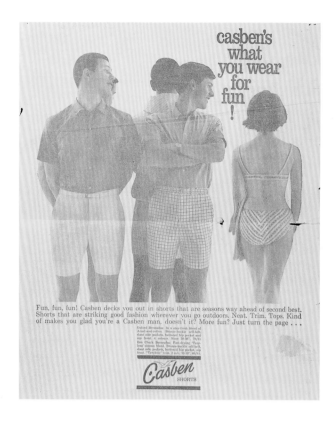

An example of Ken's early advertising artwork, featuring Ken centre front, 1963. Reproduced courtesy Kincumber Nautical Village

Judy

1960 joins Farmers department store (now Grace Brothers) as fashion style coordinator involved in developing a 'fashion look', and parades as house model

1965 leaves Farmers and travels to London to marry Ken. She features in some of Ken's advertising campaigns, works as a freelance fashion model and stylist, and studies ceramics

Wedding day, 1965.

London's the place for learning

Two young Australians have found London is for learning, but it will be home, sweet home to stay.

However, Mr and Mrs Ken Done (pictured), who arrived by Qantas yesterday from London, are not willing to come home permanently just yet.

They not only left their Chelsea flat for two months to see parents, friends and Sydney again after a three years' absence, but also to complete London business in Australia.

Mr Done is an advertising art director in London with ideas about how young Australians should arrange their business career. His wife, formerly Miss Judy Walker, of Dee Why, is a freelance model "I think it is necessary for all young Australians to travel if they wish to get ahead in business," said Mr Done.

"The easiest way to work overseas is to go to London. London is a centre for art. It has good advertising, good photography. For me, the advertising business is similar and London is also similar as a place to live.

"However, when it comes time for us to settle down, we will come home to Sydney."

After their holiday in Sydney Mr and Mrs Done will be putting Australia into English advertisements. Mrs Done, who has appeared in English "Vogue," "Nova" and a large number of English colour supplements, will model for a fashion series to be taken by an English photographer at Ayers Rock. She recently completed a similar series in Turkey.

Mr Done, who worked in Sydney and then with J. Walter Thompson in New York before going to London, will be travelling to the Barrier Reef, where he will help film advertisements underwater. This will be a continuation of another underwater series taken in Nassau 18 months ago.

Ken and Judy return to Australia for a holiday and to film some advertisements for J Walter Thompson.

In London, 1968.

. . . because Bacardi is the spirit of adventure.

Ken and Judy on underwater shoot for Bacardi Rum advertisement. Photograph by David Lowe off Lyford Cay, Nassau, Bahamas. Reproduced courtesy Bacardi-Martini Pacific

Judy (left) models Silhouette swimwear in Turkey.

1970s

Ken

1970 joins J Walter Thompson in Sydney, where he is teamed with copywriter Richard Walsh. Handles such accounts as Benson & Hedges, Rinso and Kleenex

● daughter Camilla is born

1972 appointed creative director, J Walter Thompson Sydney

1975 establishes Ken Done and Associates with writer Ken Mitchell

1976 son Oscar is born

1976–79 works as part-time creative director with Quinlon.Mitchell.Malinot and Scott, on accounts including Cussons Imperial Leather soap and Johnson & Johnson. Both daughter Camilla and son Oscar feature in some of Ken's advertising campaigns: Oscar was the Johnson & Johnson baby and Camilla appeared in Coppertone television commercials

1977 exhibits *Postcard from God*, 1975, oil on canvas, 110 x 164 cm, in the Blake Prize

1979 wins first prize in Outdoor Advertising Association of Australia's National Outdoor Advertising Competition for 24-sheet poster advertising television series *The Sullivans*

● exhibits *Australia Day 1980*, oil on canvas, 91 x 122 cm, in Sulman Prize for landscape painting, Art Gallery of New South Wales

● prints limited edition of helmet shell lithograph for sale

Judy

1970 works as model with Hunt Woodley Modelling Agency. After Camilla is born Judy continues to freelance as a model

1978–79 designs and makes evening wear, accessories and unusual knitwear for Mark and Geoffrey boutique, Double Bay, and other boutiques

Billy Blue **cover designed by Ken Done featuring** *Basket of cowries*, **1980, 36 x 50 cm.** Courtesy Billy Blue Design

Nautilus shell, **1975, pencil on paper.**

Postcard from God, exhibited in the Blake Prize at the Commonwealth Bank Gallery in 1978.

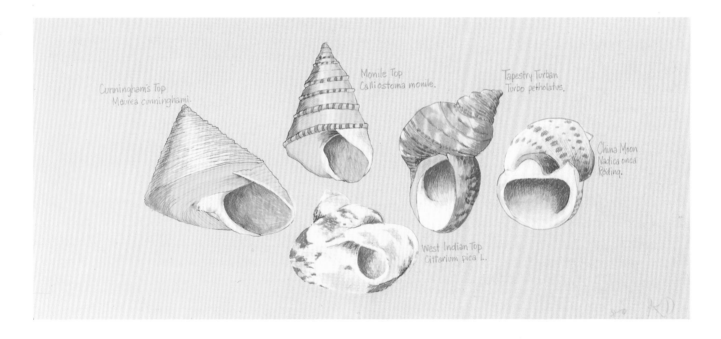

Study of five shells, 1979, watercolour, pencil and pen on grey card.

1980s

Ken

1980 rents the Cabin at Chinamans Beach as a painting studio. Holds first exhibition at the Holdsworth Galleries

● opens The Art Directors Gallery in Ridge Street, North Sydney, with a solo exhibition which he promotes with a limited edition of single-colour silkscreen 'Sydney Harbour' T-shirt

1980–83 designs fifteen covers for *Billy Blue* magazine

1981 *Ken Done 1981* and *Art from Billy Blue* exhibitions, Art Directors Gallery, North Sydney

● designs stationery, including a 1982 calendar, for The Ink Group Publishers

1982 opens The Art Directors Gallery and The Sydney Harbour Shop together at 123 George Street, The Rocks; mounts *Ken Done 1982* exhibition

● produces 'Downunder' and 'Australia' images for T-shirts and sweatshirts

● exhibits *Trying to paint on a Monday*, 1981, oil on canvas, 100 x 140 cm, in the Sulman Prize

● joins SPS Advertising as creative director; accounts include ABC Television and Radio

● wins Certificate of Creative Excellence in advertising industry CLIO awards for his illustration in Monahan Dayman Adams agency's Perrier campaign

1983 establishes Ken Done Down Under Pty Ltd as a separate entity from Ken Done and Assoc

● wins Federation of Australian Commercial Television Stations (FACTS) award for Set Design for the 'Sea House' ad for Cussons Imperial Leather soap which he wrote and directed for SPS Advertising Agents

● Australian Writers and Art Directors Silver Award is presented to The Art Directors Gallery for colour-poster illustration and to Ken Done for his typography and graphic design for The Sydney Harbour Shop, his colour posters for Ken Done and Associates, and the graphic design of letter-heads for SPS Advertising client Radio JJJ FM

● licensees of Ken Done's designs now include Summertime swimwear, Hale Imports (home-wares), Textile Industries of Australia (Sheridan

The Cabin at Chinamans Beach, 1984, oil on canvas.

Postcard from the Cabin, 1981, oil on canvas.

manchester), and Oroton International (fashion accessories)

● holds solo exhibition at Queensland College of Art Gallery, Brisbane

● exhibits his paintings, drawings, silkscreens and tapestries at The Art Directors Gallery

1984 exhibits *Beach*, 1984, oil on canvas, 130 x 129 cm, in the Sulman Prize

● exhibits *Me*, 1984, oil on canvas, 191 x 184 cm, in the Archibald Prize for portraiture, Art Gallery of New South Wales

1985 holds solo exhibition of *Nudes and Limited Editions* at The Art Directors Gallery

● solo exhibition, Chapman Gallery, Canberra

● solo exhibition, Bonython–Meadmore Gallery, Adelaide

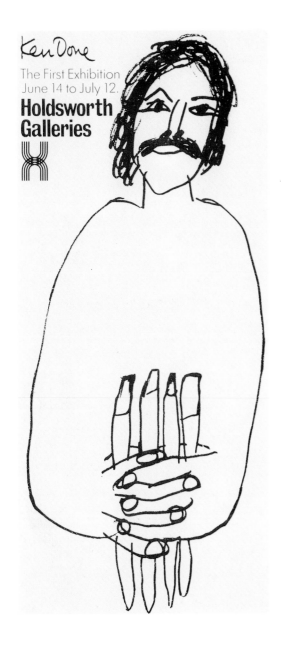

Ken Done
The First Exhibition
June 14 to July 12.
**Holdsworth
Galleries**

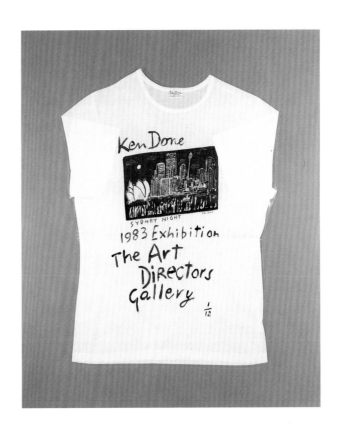

Limited-edition T-shirt featuring *Sydney night* produced for 1983 exhibition at The Art Directors Gallery.

Invitation to Ken's first solo exhibition, 1980.
Reproduced courtesy Holdsworth Galleries

• exhibits *Manly morning*, 1985, oil on canvas, 215 x 304 cm, in the Sulman Prize

1986 solo exhibition, Gallery Tamon, Tokyo

• wins New South Wales Department of Tourism award for Tourism Marketing

• commissioned to design glassware for Swedish company Kosta Boda

1987 exhibits *Talking to Sir Sidney Nolan*, 1987, oil on canvas, 92 x 196 cm, in the Sulman Prize

• highly commended in the FACTS Awards, category Alcoholic Beverages, for his ads for Carlton & United Brewery

• solo exhibitions, Black Swan Gallery, Fremantle; Bonython–Meadmore Gallery, Adelaide; Chapman Gallery, Canberra; and in Mt Gambier, Victoria, and Orange, NSW

Ken models his first Sydney T-shirt.

1988 opens Moore Park Gallery, Sydney

● appointed a goodwill ambassador for UNICEF

● designs facade of the Australian Pavilion at World Expo in Brisbane in 1988

● finalist in the BHP Pursuit of Excellence 1988, category: Commerce, Industry and Management

● contracted to create artworks for the covers of a new Japanese weekly magazine, *Hanako*

In 1988, Hanako, a life-related information magazine for young women working in the Tokyo metropolitan area, was launched. From the very inauguration issue, the magazine's cover has been uninterruptedly graced by Ken Done's work. Chairman Tatsuo Shimizu of Magazine House, the publisher of Hanako, believes that a new periodical has more than an 80 per cent success ratio if a truly appropriate artist is chosen to do its cover. Ken Done has amply shown the correctness of Mr Shimizu's belief. — Yamato Shine, previous editor of *Hanako*, 'Happiness of the Southern Hemisphere', in catalogue, *Ken Done major exhibition*, Japan, 1991, © 1991 *Yomiuri Shimbun*

● solo exhibitions at Bridgewater Mill, Adelaide, and Seibu Ikebukuro Art Gallery, Tokyo

1989 commissioned by BMW to paint a car exhibited at the Powerhouse Museum, Sydney

● named Father of the Year

● Done family visits Africa for UNICEF

● solo exhibitions at Chapman Gallery, Canberra; Moore Park Gallery, Sydney

● exhibits casual clothing and accessories in Australian section, World Fashion Fair, Osaka; shows oil paintings, silkscreens and objects in solo exhibition, Laforet Museum, Tokyo

Judy

1984 enters into partnership with Zuccala boutique, Woollahra and later Double Bay

1986 joins Ken Done Down Under as a designer and develops a ready-to-wear range as all manufacture presently licensed out — except that for Oroton International and The Ink Group Publishers — is brought in-house

1988 Done Art and Design designs staff uniforms for World Expo 1988 in Brisbane

● fashion house Simona releases the first range under the Judy Done label

Done outside The Art Directors Gallery, 123 George Street, The Rocks, about 1985.

Test issue *Hanako* cover. Reproduced courtesy Magazine House, Tokyo

Judy Done's first fashion range — Judy Done by Simona.

'Art car' painted by Ken Done for BMW; exhibited in *Art cars*, Powerhouse Museum, Sydney, 1989. Courtesy BMW

1990s

Ken

1990 exhibits *Meeting Michael Jagamara Nelson*, 1989, oil and acrylic on canvas, 102 x 198 cm, in Archibald Prize

• solo travelling exhibition *Ken Done: painting 1980–90* in Japan — Aces Gallery, Tokyo; Amics Gallery, Tokyo; Art Gallery of Yokahama Takashimaya; Ciel Gallery, Tochigi; Gallery Tamon, Tokyo; in Australia — Caulfield Arts Complex, Melbourne; Geelong Art Gallery; Mildura Art Gallery; Campbelltown City Art Gallery

• invited to design a limited-edition Arnott's biscuit tin. Proceeds of its sale donated to UNICEF

1991 designs a can for the Japanese brewer Suntory's Australian-hops beer

• Shinsegae Gallery, Seoul, holds a Ken Done promotion

• solo travelling exhibition *Ken Done major exhibition*, Japan 1991, goes to Tokyo, Umeda, Osaka, Shimonoseki, Fukuoka and Nagasaki

• commissioned by Keihan Electric Railway Co, Japan, to complete promotional artwork for a new town, East Rosetown

1991–93 solo travelling exhibition *Ken Done direct from Japan* goes to Manly Art Gallery & Museum; Lewers Bequest, Penrith Regional Gallery; Tamworth City Art Gallery; Moree Plains Gallery; Orange Regional Gallery; Lake Macquarie City Art Gallery; Grafton Art Gallery; and Broken Hill City Art Gallery

1992 made a member of the Order of Australia for services to art, design and tourism

• Done Art and Design established as a trading name and company

1993 solo exhibition *A new decade: recent work by Ken Done* at Moore Park Gallery, Sydney, and Ken Done galleries, The Rocks, Sydney, and Surfers Paradise, Queensland

• exhibits *Glenn Murcutt*, 1992, acrylic on canvas, 152 x 114 cm, in Archibald Prize

• exhibits *Balmoral Sunday*, 1993, oil and acrylic on canvas, 153 x 114 cm, in Wynn Prize

• exhibits *Walking on the waterline*, 1993, gouche, oil crayon and ink on paper, 45 x 60 cm, in Dobell Prize

Cover of Australian catalogue for the touring exhibition *Direct from Japan*.

Done visits Vietnam as a goodwill ambassador for UNICEF.
Photograph by Peter Solness/Wildlight

Catalogue for opening exhibition at the new Ken Done Gallery in Hickson Road, The Rocks.

Judy at the 1993 Australian Fashion Awards. Reproduced courtesy Fashion Industries of Australia

- travels to Vietnam as goodwill ambassador for UNICEF, accompanied by photographer Peter Solness

- solo exhibition *Beneath the surface: underwater works by Ken Done* at Moore Park Gallery and Ken Done Gallery, Sydney

Ken has dared to tread where others have not, to take Australia as he sees it and market it to the rest of the world. Art, or fashion? What is the difference, when the result is an extremely appealing piece of clothing?

Can you name one other person throughout the world who has done what Ken Done has? To take one's country and draw on it for inspiration and give it an individual twist? I believe he is unique in this field, and it's about time he received the public recognition he deserves.

I believe he has contributed enormously to the recognition of Australian fashion design around the world, and is a wonderful ambassador, whose fierce love and loyalty for his country is inspiring.
— Adele Palmer, *The Age*, 14 September 1993

1994 creates the interior for the Garden Restaurant for the Powerhouse Museum, Sydney

- exhibits *Reef*, 1994, acrylic and oil on canvas, 214 x 198 cm, in Sulman Prize

- opens Ken Done Gallery, Hickson Road, The Rocks, with joint exhibition with Peter Solness, *Journey to Viet Nam*

- made a Paul Harris Fellow by Rotary International

- Powerhouse Museum, Sydney, holds exhibition *Ken Done: the art of design*

Judy

1990 designs for first swimwear range produced for Done Art and Design

1991 releases first resort-wear collection comprising a trans-seasonal range with an Australian theme

- works with master jeweller Peter Meier to design a range of jewellery inspired by Ken's Barrier Reef series of paintings

1993 accepts Fashion Industries of Australia Grand Award for outstanding achievement in original design and export for Done Art and Design

- launches winter 1993 and summer 1993–94 collections. Winter collection uses innovative printing techniques on woollen fabrics

About the authors

Terence Measham was appointed director of the Powerhouse Museum in 1988. His previous appointments were with the Tate Gallery, London, in the 1970s and the National Gallery of Australia, Canberra, in the 1980s. He has been published widely on modern international art and Australian art and design. His most recent publication is the book *Treasures of the Powerhouse Museum*, published in 1994.

Reinosuke Hara is the vice president of Seiko Instruments Inc in Japan, which specialises in developing innovative electronic instruments, information devices and systems. Ken Done has been involved in numerous projects with Dr Hara and Seiko.

Anne-Marie van de Ven, a curator of Australian decorative arts and design at the Powerhouse Museum, has special responsibility for graphic design and commercial photography. She is the author of numerous articles on architectural and interior decoration and graphic design and the co-curator of *Gordon Andrews: a retrospective* held at the Powerhouse Museum in 1993–94.

Yoshihisa Kinameri is president of Magazine House, a major Japanese publisher whose titles include the weekly magazine *Hanako* and *Hanako West*, a monthly offshoot serving the Osaka area.

Richard Wood, curator of production design and marketing at the Powerhouse Museum, is also a children's writer and a television presenter. He has spent the past nine years championing Australian innovation in design and industry through exhibitions, books and the electronic media.

Machi Tawara is an award-winning Japanese poet whose collections of poetry have been best-sellers in Japan. Ms Tawara also writes cultural criticism for major newspapers in Japan.

Donna Lee Brien is a curator and historian with a special interest in biography. Her previous publications include essays on the artist and arts benefactor John Power and on various contemporary Australian artists. Donna is currently curator of art and special projects coordinator for Ken Done.

Elizabeth Buzby is the assistant curator at the Powerhouse Museum for the *Ken Done: the art of design* exhibition. Her special interest is decorative arts, particularly Asian textiles, and she has taught textiles and design in secondary schools.

S.C.E.C.G.S. REDLANDS

R19384M ROSE

031194

759.994
DON